Incarnations

An Oracle Guidebook

J Edward Neill & Heather Reiter

All Art by J Edward Neill

Téssera
A Creative Guild

Welcome to Dreams & Incarnations. This 52-card oracle deck includes original art by artist J Edward Neill and guidebook by Heather Neill.

Dreams & Incarnations is our second oracle deck. Our focus this time is awareness of both the conscious (waking) and subconscious (dreaming) self. We seek to illuminate the abstract qualities of the human experience, while at the same time give voice to the realm of the sleeping mind. It's our hope this deck will offer clarity to those who seek it.

Herein you'll discover dreamlike, surreal images, meant to guide viewers between the wakeful and sleeping worlds. You'll discover dream cards (reflective of common dream states) and incarnations (reflective of personalities you may encounter or become while dreaming or in real life.)

Dreams & Incarnations is an intuitive deck. The keywords and meaning for each card are merely starting points. Please take the time to connect to each image in a meaningful way.

This deck was made for you.

ABANDONMENT

ABANDONMENT

KEYWORDS: LONELINESS, NEGLECT, FORGOTTEN

ABANDONMENT COMMUNICATES THE FEAR OF BEING LEFT BEHIND OR LEFT ALONE. YOU MAY FEEL THAT SOMEONE IN YOUR LIFE HAS MOVED ON AND FORGOTTEN YOU OR, CONVERSELY, YOU MAY FEEL YOU HAVE MOVED FORWARD AND ABANDONED SOMEONE OR SOMETHING IN YOUR LIFE.

ABANDONMENT CAN ALSO BE THE FEAR OF A WRONGDOING COMING TO LIGHT OR THE DISCOVERY OF AN INDISCRETION THAT LEADS TO DISSOLVED RELATIONSHIPS.

YOU MAY FEEL THAT YOU ARE BEING NEGLECTED OR IGNORED BY SOMEONE CLOSE TO YOU.

BETRAYAL

BETRAYAL

KEYWORDS: DECEPTION, SUSPICION, INFIDELITY

BETRAYAL SUGGESTS THAT TRUST HAS BEEN BROKEN. YOU MAY SUSPECT THAT SOMEONE CLOSE TO YOU HAS BEEN UNRELIABLE AND BROKEN THE PROMISES THAT THEY MADE TO YOU. BETRAYAL CAN ALSO ILLUMINATE THE FEAR OF INFIDELITY IN A RELATIONSHIP BUT NOT NECESSARILY THE ACT OF BEING UNFAITHFUL.

BETRAYAL MAY REVEAL THAT YOU HAVE BEEN DISLOYAL TO YOURSELF BY IGNORING YOUR NEEDS OR WISHES AND CONSEQUENTLY PREVENTING YOUR OWN HAPPINESS.

CORRIDOR

CORRIDOR

KEYWORDS: CHOICES, ACCESS, UNDISCOVERED

CORRIDOR CAN BE A PASSAGE, ALLEY, OR HALLWAY. IT IS A CONNECTION TO THE DIFFERENT AREAS OF THE INNER SELF (REPRESENTED BY THE HOUSE). DOORS ALONG THE WAY OR AT THE END OF THE CORRIDOR, ESPECIALLY IF THEY ARE CLOSED, LOCKED, OR OTHERWISE INACCESSIBLE, CAN LEAD TO UNDISCOVERED ROOMS OF THE SELF OR UNEXPLORED AREAS IN LIFE.

THE CORRIDOR CAN ALSO SYMBOLIZE THE FEELING OF BEING CONSTRICTED DUE TO THE BELIEF THAT YOU HAVE LIMITED POSSIBILITIES IN YOUR LIFE. EXPLORE THE DIFFERENT AREAS OF THE CORRIDOR TO DISCOVER THAT YOU HAVE MORE OPTIONS THAN YOU REALIZE.

DECAY

DECAY

KEYWORDS: POWERLESS, WORRY, WARNING

DECAY REVEALS A FEELING OF POWERLESSNESS. IN DREAMS, DECAY (INCLUDING LOST OR LOOSE TEETH) CAN INDICATE POWERFUL WORRY OR ANXIETY OVER A CURRENT SITUATION. AN AILING PART OF THE BODY CAN BE A WARNING TO TEND TO CERTAIN AREAS OF YOUR LIFE THAT YOU MAY HAVE NEGLECTED.

DECAY CAN ALSO BE A REMINDER TO TAKE TIME FOR SELF-CARE. BE MINDFUL OF THE WAY YOU TEND TO YOUR PHYSICAL, EMOTIONAL, AND SPIRITUAL HEALTH.

DESIRE

DESIRE

KEYWORDS: CONNECTION, RELEASE, STIMULATION

DESIRE INDICATES A NEED FOR CONNECTION ON A PHYSICAL
OR MENTAL LEVEL.

DREAMS OF DESIRE MAY BE PHYSICAL AND REVEAL THE
NEED TO RELEASE SEXUAL TENSION. THEY MAY ALSO CARRY
THE MESSAGE THAT A PHYSICAL CONNECTION IS MISSING IN
YOUR LIFE.

DESIRE CAN ALSO INDICATE A NEED FOR MENTAL
STIMULATION THAT CAN BE FOUND BY CONNECTING
INTELLECTUALLY WITH OTHERS.

DYSTOPIA

KEYWORDS: REMOTE, ISOLATED, DISCONNECTED

SLEEPING OR WAKEFUL THOUGHTS OF DYSTOPIAN IMAGES AND MOODS CAN BE POWERFUL, SOMETIMES EVEN DEBILITATING. VISIONS OF ONESELF IN LONELY OR EMPTY PLACES CONVEY THE SENSE OF NOT BELONGING OR DISCONNECTION FROM PLACES WHICH FEEL LIKE HOME. A DYSTOPIAN WORLD OFTEN SYMBOLIZES FEELINGS OF ISOLATION.

DWELLING TOO LONG IN SUCH MOODS CAN LEAD TO A SENSE OF DIMINISHED MEANING. BE MINDFUL NOT TO LINGER.

FALLING

KEYWORDS: FRAGILE, UNCERTAIN, WITHDRAWAL

FALLING CAN SYMBOLIZE DEEP UNCERTAINTY ABOUT ONE'S SAFETY OR SECURITY. IT MAY REVEAL THE FEAR THAT THE COMFORT OF A SUPPORT SYSTEM OR SAFETY NET, SUCH AS FRIENDSHIP, FAMILY, OR ROMANTIC LOVE, WILL BE WITHDRAWN.

DREAMS OF TUMBLING HELPLESSLY THROUGH THE SKY ARE COMMON, OFTEN INSPIRING A VERY PRIMAL TERROR, BUT RARELY IS THE ISSUE AN ACTUAL FEAR OF FALLING. ALMOST ALWAYS, THE TRUE FEAR IS EMOTIONAL, NOT PHYSICAL. SEARCH YOUR HEART AND FIND THE THING WHICH WILL RESTORE SECURITY TO YOUR LIFE.

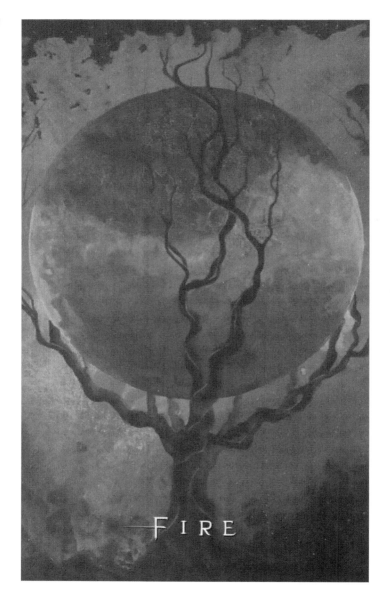

FIRE

Fire

KEYWORDS: INTENSE, FRENETIC, DISCONTENT

Fire represents intensity or passion. A frenetic fire indicates unfocused emotions or passions that can cause a general feeling of dissatisfaction.

You may seek completion from an external source rather than looking within yourself to find lasting contentment. Do not burn others in your attempt to find satisfaction, but instead direct the fire towards personally satisfying pursuits. A controlled, steady flame keeps the passion burning.

FLYING

KEYWORDS: UNBOUND, EXPLORATION, ESCAPE

WHETHER ASLEEP OR AWAKE, THE FEELING OF SOARING THROUGH THE SKY CAN MAKE ONE FEEL UNBOUND, EVEN UNTOUCHABLE. —FLYING REPRESENTS THE LONGING TO ESCAPE THE ORDINARY OR MUNDANE ROUTINE OF DAILY LIFE. IT REVEALS READINESS FOR SOMETHING NEW — AN EXCITING CHANGE OR A NEW ADVENTURE.

—FLYING CAN UNCOVER THE WISH TO ABANDON A PROBLEM OR OBSTACLE THAT IS HOLDING YOU BACK. TO BETTER VISUALIZE THAT WHICH HINDERS YOU, SOAR HIGH ABOVE IT.

Freedom

KEYWORDS: HORSE, LIBERATION, MOVEMENT

THE HORSE SYMBOLIZES FREEDOM. IT EXPRESSES THE LONGING TO BE UNRESTRAINED OR TO BREAK FREE FROM CONFINEMENT.

THE HORSE CAN ALSO COMMUNICATE THE NEED FOR PHYSICAL MOVEMENT OR RELOCATION. YOU MAY FEEL THAT YOU LACK THE FREEDOM OR SPACE TO BE AUTHENTIC AND TRUE TO YOURSELF.

OPPORTUNITIES FOR FREEDOM TEND TO BE FEW AND FAR BETWEEN. EMBRACE THEM WHENEVER YOU CAN.

GUARDIAN

GUARDIAN

KEYWORDS: CROCODILE, ENTRANCE, THRESHOLD

IN THE DREAM REALM, THE CROCODILE IS THE GUARDIAN TO THE ENTRANCE OF THE SUBCONSCIOUS. PULLING THE GUARDIAN CARD INDICATES A NEED TO CROSS OVER INTO PARTS OF YOUR INNER SELF THAT HAVE BEEN INACCESSIBLE OR GUARDED FROM YOUR WAKING MIND.

SELF-PERMISSION IS NEEDED TO CROSS THE THRESHOLD INTO UNEXPLORED TERRITORIES OF THE PSYCHE IN ORDER TO FIND THE ANSWERS YOU SEEK.

HOUSE

HOUSE

KEYWORDS: PSYCHE, SECRETS, DISCOVERY

HOUSE REPRESENTS THE INNER SELF OR PSYCHE. IN DREAMS, THE ROOMS IN A HOUSE REPRESENT DIFFERENT AREAS OF THE SUBCONSCIOUS. RECURRING DREAMS OF A HOUSE INDICATE THAT YOUR SUBCONSCIOUS IS ASKING YOU TO EXPLORE EACH ROOM AND UNCOVER ALL HIDDEN AREAS, DISCOVERING THE SECRETS WITHIN.

THE ATMOSPHERE OR CONDITION OF THE ROOMS WILL BRING INSIGHT INTO THE MIND. DARKNESS OR LIGHT, ANY SCENTS, AND ALL APPEARANCES SHOULD BE NOTED.

THE HOUSE MAY CONTAIN HALLWAYS, DOORS, BARRIERS, GUARDIANS, WINDOWS, EVEN THE SENSE OF A PRESENCE. DOES THE PRESENCE FEEL COMFORTABLY FAMILIAR OR OMINOUS? PREVIOUSLY UNDISCOVERED AREAS WILL LIKELY FEEL UNCOMFORTABLE AT FIRST.

DISCOVERING UNTRAVERSED PARTS OF YOUR PSYCHE CAN LEAD TO A BETTER UNDERSTANDING OF YOURSELF, YOUR MOTIVATIONS, AND WHAT BRINGS PERSONAL HAPPINESS INTO YOUR LIFE.

INSTINCT

KEYWORDS: WOLF, DRIVE, UNTAMED

THE WOLF SYMBOLIZES INSTINCT AND THE WILLINGNESS TO STRIDE TOWARDS A GOAL WITHOUT FEAR OR SECOND-GUESSING ONESELF.

THE WOLF RARELY STOPS TO OVERTHINK OR GET LOST IN FEELINGS. INSTEAD OF TIPTOEING TOWARD THAT WHICH YOU DESIRE, TAP INTO YOUR GUT INSTINCT AND LEAP FORWARD WITH CONFIDENCE.

IN LIFE, CAUTION MUST SOMETIMES BE TOSSED ASIDE AND FEARLESSNESS EMBRACED.

MARRIAGE

MARRIAGE

KEYWORDS: HARMONY, UNIFICATION, BEGINNING

MARRIAGE IS SYMBOLIC OF A BENEFICIAL UNION. IT MAY REPRESENT A PROMISING AGREEMENT BETWEEN YOU AND SOMEONE ELSE, A CONTRACT, OR AN ADVANTAGEOUS NEW PARTNERSHIP.

MARRIAGE REPRESENTS THE NEED FOR UNIFICATION OF THE SELF. AT TIMES, WE MAY FEEL TORN BETWEEN TWO THINGS AND FIND OURSELVES STRUGGLING TO MAKE A DECISION. TAKE THE TIME TO SIT AND MEDITATE ON WHAT YOU TRULY WANT.

MARRIAGE CAN ALSO FORETELL THE BEGINNING OF A NEW ROMANTIC RELATIONSHIP.

MASK

MASK

KEYWORDS: GUISE, CONCEALED, IDENTITY

MASK IS A GUISE USED TO CONCEAL ONE'S TRUE IDENTITY. IT CAN BE A PERSONA THAT HAS BEEN CONSTRUCTED DUE TO THE NEED FOR SELF-PRESERVATION, OR AN ANTICIPATED NEED FOR A TEMPORARY CHANGE IN PERSONALITY DUE TO SPECIFIC CIRCUMSTANCES.

MASK MAY ALSO BE USED TO HIDE FEELINGS OF VULNERABILITY. EMBRACE YOUR VULNERABILITY. DO NOT WASTE TIME HIDING YOUR GENUINE SELF BENEATH AN INSINCERE MASK.

MESSENGER

MESSENGER

KEYWORDS: CORVID, ENLIGHTEN, TRUTH

CORVIDS, SUCH AS RAVENS, CROWS, AND MAGPIES, ARE TRUTH TELLERS THAT BRING MESSAGES FROM INACCESSIBLE AREAS OF THE SUBCONSCIOUS. IN DREAMS THEY MAY BRING OBJECTS WITH THEM TO CONVEY THEIR MESSAGE, SMALL TRINKETS WHICH CARRY MUCH GREATER MEANING.

WISE AND CUNNING, MESSENGERS CAN DELIVER IDEAS AND ANSWERS ACROSS RIVERS OF THOUGHT THAT MIGHT OTHERWISE BE IMPASSABLE. THOUGH AT FIRST THEIR MESSAGE MAY SEEM CLOUDED, IT'S KEY TO REMEMBER THAT THE JOURNEY OF DISCOVERING LIFE'S MEANINGS IS OFTEN AS IMPORTANT (IF NOT MORE SO) THAN THE MEANINGS THEMSELVES.

LOOK CAREFULLY AND FIND WHAT YOU SEEK.

MORTALITY

KEYWORDS: CHANGE, —FEAR, AGING

MORTALITY IS CHANGE OR THE FEAR OF CHANGE. THESE
FEARS OFTEN EMERGE FROM THE CONCERN THAT
SOMETHING IMPORTANT MAY BE LOST, AND FROM
AVERSION TO THE RISKS ONE MUST TAKE IN ORDER TO
ASCEND OR SUCCEED.

EXAMPLES OF CHANGE ARE: ENDING OF A PHASE IN LIFE,
LETTING GO OF A FRIENDSHIP, FAMILY MEMBER, OR
RELATIONSHIP, OR EVEN THE PROCESS OF GROWING OLDER.

WE HAVE LIMITED TIME GIVEN TO US IN OUR LIVES, AND
ALTHOUGH THE PATH IS PERILOUS, THE ONLY WAY TO
BECOME OUR BEST SELVES IS TO SET ASIDE OUR MOST BASIC
OF FEARS — DEATH.

PEACE

PEACE

KEYWORDS: DOVE, RESTORATION, RECONCILIATION

THE DOVE REPRESENTS PEACE AND RECONCILIATION. IT COMMUNICATES THE GENTLE HUMILITY THAT IS NECESSARY TO ELIMINATE CONFLICT AND RESTORE FRACTURED RELATIONSHIPS.

LETTING DOWN YOUR GUARD AND BEING THE ONE TO EXTEND AN OLIVE BRANCH TAKES COURAGE. THE DOVE COMMUNICATES THE NEED TO BE OPEN TO HEARING ANOTHER PERSON'S POINT OF VIEW IN ORDER TO ELIMINATE CONFLICT.

POWER

POWER

KEYWORDS: BEAR, FORMIDABLE, WILLPOWER

THE BEAR IS THE POWER OF MIND AND WILL TO ACHIEVE ANYTHING. WITH THE STRENGTH AND COURAGE OF A STOUT HEART, EVERY OUTCOME BECOMES POSSIBLE. DREAMS OR EVEN DAYDREAMS OF POWERFUL CREATURES, EVEN IF THEY SEEM FRIGHTENING ON THE SURFACE, CAN CONVEY A HIDDEN INTENSITY OR DEEPER POWER WITHIN THE DREAMER'S MIND.

WHEN POWER AND SELF-AWARENESS COME TOGETHER, ONE CAN REALIZE ONE'S SUPREME CAPABILITY. THROW ASIDE YOUR FEARS. TAKE WHAT IS RIGHTFULLY YOURS.

PURSUIT

PURSUIT

KEYWORDS: CHASE, EVADE, HIDE

PURSUIT IS THE DESIRE TO FLEE FROM SOMETHING OR SOMEONE. (AVOIDING OR HIDING FROM A PERSON, SITUATION, OR RESPONSIBILITY.) ALTERNATIVELY, IT CAN ALSO REVEAL YOU ARE CHASING SOMETHING OR SOMEONE, LIKELY A MOVING TARGET, IN AN ATTEMPT TO OBTAIN ANSWERS OR CLOSURE.

WHEN BEING PURSUED IN LIFE, SOMETIMES IT'S BEST TO LOOK CLOSELY AT THE PURSUER. BE IT A PERSON OR AN OPPORTUNITY, THE CHOICE WILL OFTEN BECOME — CONTINUE FLEEING (AVOIDING CONFRONTATION) OR ALLOW ONESELF TO BE CAUGHT (FACING ONE'S FEARS DIRECTLY.)

IN THE CASE OF CHASING ONE'S DESIRES, THE BEST QUESTION TO ASK ONESELF BECOMES — "DO I REALLY, TRULY WANT WHAT I'M CHASING?" REMEMBER TO BE CAREFUL WHAT YOU WISH FOR.

SEARCHING

SEARCHING

KEYWORDS: RESTLESS, DISSATISFIED, ABSENCE

SEARCHING IS THE FEELING THAT SOMETHING IS ABSENT IN YOUR LIFE. WHETHER DREAMED OR DAYDREAMED OF, WHAT YOU SEEK MAY BE VEILED IN SHADOW. OR IT MAY BE THAT YOUR DESIRE IS KNOWN, BUT UNATTAINABLE AT THE PRESENT MOMENT IN YOUR LIFE.

SEARCHING MAY ALSO BE A FEELING OF RESTLESSNESS THAT PERVADES YOUR LIFE AND CAUSES YOU TO FEEL DISSATISFIED. IF ALLOWED TO LINGER, THIS SENSE OF DISQUIET CAN DISRUPT ONE'S SENSE OF SELF.

REMEMBER THAT ALTHOUGH DISCOVERING A PURPOSE CAN LEAD TO CONTENTMENT, THE SEARCH CANNOT BE RUSHED. PATIENCE AND OPEN-MINDEDNESS WILL ALLOW ONE TO BE READY WHEN THE DREAMED-OF MOMENT ARRIVES.

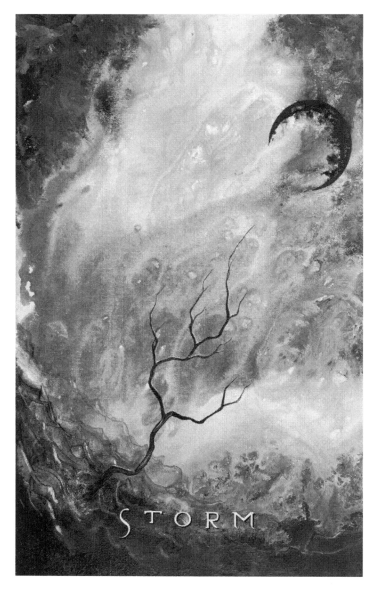

STORM

STORM

KEYWORDS: UNCONTROLLABLE, OVERWHELM, CHAOS

STORM IS FEELING OVERWHELMED BY EMOTIONAL CHAOS, EITHER YOUR OWN OR ANOTHER PERSON'S. BEING CAUGHT IN A STORM IS FEELING YOU HAVE LITTLE CONTROL OVER WHAT IS HAPPENING AROUND YOU.

STRONG FEELINGS MAY FEEL UNMANAGEABLE, AND YOU MAY FEEL POWERLESS AS THE TEMPEST SURROUNDS YOU. STAY CENTERED AND REMEMBER THAT ALL STORMS WILL PASS.

TEARS

TEARS

KEYWORDS: CATHARSIS, HEALING, SOLACE

TEARS INDICATES THE NEED FOR HEALING OR CATHARSIS. THE PROCESS OF LETTING GO OF IMPRISONED EMOTIONS BRINGS MUCH NEEDED RELIEF.

TEARS CAN ALSO REPRESENT THE NEED FOR PURIFICATION BY CLEANSING YOURSELF OF EMOTIONS OR THOUGHTS THAT ARE NOT USEFUL AND DO NOT PROMOTE WELLBEING. MEDITATION OR A QUIET WALK SURROUNDED BY NATURE CAN HELP CLEAR YOUR MIND OF TROUBLESOME THOUGHTS. RELEASING STAGNANT, UNCOMFORTABLE EMOTIONS THROUGH TEARS CAN BRING MUCH NEEDED SOLACE.

TERROR

TERROR

KEYWORDS: HIDDEN, REPRESSION, AVOIDANCE

IN MOST CASES, TERROR IS UNEXAMINED OR UNRELEASED EMOTIONS. IN DREAMS, NIGHTMARES ARE THE SUBCONSCIOUS'S WAY OF BRINGING THESE FEELINGS TO LIGHT. THESE FEARSOME VISIONS WILL OFTEN ARRIVE SUDDENLY AND UNEXPECTEDLY, AND WILL GENERATE A RAW AND PRIMAL SENSE OF FEAR.

TERROR MAY ALSO REPRESENT THE INABILITY TO PROCESS A SITUATION IN A TIME OF CRISIS. WHEN PRESSURE MOUNTS, THE HUMAN MIND WILL OFTEN PANIC AND RETREAT INTO SHADOW. TO OVERCOME THESE HELPLESS FEELINGS, ASK YOURSELF — "WHAT IS AT THE ROOT OF THIS? —FROM WHERE INSIDE ME DOES THIS FEAR ARISE?"

THE
ALCHEMIST

THE ALCHEMIST

KEYWORDS: TRANSMUTE, ALTER, PERFECT

IN THE ALCHEMIST'S VIEW, THE WORLD IS ALWAYS IN NEED OF
IMPROVEMENT. THE ALCHEMIST TRANSMUTES ENERGY, FEELINGS,
THOUGHTS, AND CIRCUMSTANCES FOR THE BETTER, OR AT LEAST,
ATTEMPTS TO DO SO. IF A MINDSET, RELATIONSHIP, OR EVEN THE
PHYSICAL WORLD CAN BE ALTERED OR OUTRIGHT REIMAGINED, IT
WILL BE.

AND YET, NOT ALL THINGS ARE MEANT TO BE PERFECTED. MUCH OF
THE HUMAN EXPERIENCE IS BEST LEFT TO OCCUR NATURALLY,
UNFILTERED AND UNCHANGED, EVEN WHEN THE RESULTS ARE
UNPREDICTABLE.

THE ALCHEMIST OFFERS US THE OPPORTUNITY TO MAKE THE WORLD
A BETTER PLACE, BUT MUST BE BALANCED BY AVOIDING
MANIPULATION.

THE
ANCESTOR

THE ANCESTOR

KEYWORDS: REMEMBRANCE, ROOTS, APPRECIATION

THE ANCESTOR CARRIES THE ENERGY OF THOSE WHO HAVE WALKED BEFORE US.

THE ANCESTOR COMMUNICATES A NEED TO CONNECT TO YOUR ROOTS. A CELEBRATION OF EARLIER GENERATIONS, AND EVEN THOSE WHO WILL COME AFTER YOU, IS A WAY OF HONORING LOVED ONES AND REVERING LINEAGE.

THE ANCESTOR CAN COMMUNICATE THE NEED TO RESOLVE ISSUES BETWEEN YOURSELF AND A LOVED ONE WHO HAS PASSED. FORGIVING A WRONGDOING THAT WAS DONE TO YOU, OR IF NECESSARY, FORGIVING YOURSELF, BRINGS MUCH NEEDED PEACE TO YOUR FAMILY LINE.

WHILE PRESERVING ANCESTRAL CUSTOMS AND ATTITUDES IS RESPECTFUL, SOMETIMES DOING SO CAN HINDER PROGRESSION IN THE PRESENT DAY. DO NOT FIND YOURSELF STUCK IN "OLD" WAYS IF THEY ARE LIMITING OR CONFLICT WITH YOUR OWN THOUGHTS AND BELIEFS.

THE CHILD

KEYWORDS: PLAYFUL, IMAGINATIVE, HELPLESS

THE CHILD IS THE EPITOME OF JOY. SEEING INFINITE POTENTIAL IN THE WORLD, THE CHILD UNAPOLOGETICALLY EMBRACES THE POSSIBILITIES IN LIFE. THE FREEDOM OF BEING A CHILD ALLOWS THE IMAGINATION TO FLOURISH.

THE CHILD MAY CHOOSE TO REMAIN SEEN AS SMALL OR HELPLESS AND HOLD ONTO IMMATURE BELIEFS IN ORDER TO KEEP FROM FULLY EMBRACING THE RESPONSIBILITIES OF ADULTHOOD. VIEWING ONESELF AS LACKING CERTAIN SKILLS OR BEING INCAPABLE OF FUNCTIONING AS AN INDEPENDENT ADULT PREVENTS LIVING LIFE TO ITS FULLEST POTENTIAL.

HARNESSING THE ATTRIBUTES OF THE CHILD, ALLOWING YOUR IMAGINATION TO RUN FREE, AND REMAINING YOUNG AT HEART WHILE EMBRACING THE RESPONSIBILITIES OF ADULTHOOD LEAD TO A BALANCED LIFE.

THE
DECEIVER

THE DECEIVER

KEYWORDS: MANIPULATION, PRETENSE, BURDEN

THE DECEIVER, AS THE NAME IMPLIES, IS NEVER WHO THEY PRETEND TO BE. LIES AND FABRICATIONS MERELY SKIM THE SURFACE OF THE HUMAN EFFORT TO CONTROL OUR SURROUNDINGS. THE DECEPTION OF LOVED ONES IS TO BE AVOIDED, BUT THE EVEN GRAVER SIN IS LYING TO OURSELVES.

WHAT THE DECEIVER TRULY RISKS IS NOT SIMPLY BEING CAUGHT IN A LIE. IF THE TRUTH IS BURIED SO DEEP THAT THE INNERMOST SELF LOSES TOUCH WITH ITSELF, THE DECEIVER RISKS THE GREATEST DECEPTION OF ALL — THE PRETENSE OF LIVING IN A WORLD WHICH IS NOT REAL.

IF WE STRIVE TO APPEAR AS SOMEONE OTHER THAN WHO WE TRULY ARE, WE MAY LOSE OUR VERY IDENTITY.

THE
DEFENDER

THE DEFENDER

KEYWORDS: ADVOCATE, REFORMER, ENABLER

THE DEFENDER, CHAMPION OF THE PEOPLE, SPEAKS AND ACTS ON BEHALF OF OTHERS WITH A DESIRE FOR JUSTICE. SUCH A PERSON MAY TAKE MANY FORMS: ADVOCATE, CARETAKER, LAWYER, SOLDIER...THERE IS NO LIMIT. WHEN WIELDED FROM A DESIRE TO SERVE, AND WHEN TEMPERED WITH AN UNSELFISH APPROACH, THE DEFENDER IS AMONG THE NOBLEST OF INCARNATIONS.

HOWEVER, IF THE DEFENDER'S PRIDE SHOULD BLOSSOM, OR IF THE DESIRE FOR JUSTICE GIVES WAY TO PURSUIT OF POWER, THE FALL COULD BE CATASTROPHIC.

THE DEFENDER GIVES US THE OPPORTUNITY TO SERVE SOMETHING GREATER THAN OURSELVES.

THE
DOE

THE DOE

KEYWORDS: BENEVOLENT, NURTURING, PERCEPTIVE

ABOVE ALL ELSE, THE DOE IS A NURTURER. BENEVOLENT AND WATCHFUL, SHE IS THE CARETAKER OF OTHER LIVING CREATURES. THE DOE'S GENTLE PRESENCE AND SUPPORTIVE NATURE REPRESENTS UNCONDITIONAL LOVE AND LIFE-GIVING ENERGY.

IF THE DOE FOCUSES ON HER OWN DESIRE TO BE NEEDED, SEEING IT AS ESSENTIAL FOR HER HAPPINESS, SHE CAN BECOME SMOTHERING OR OVER-PROTECTIVE. THE DOE CAN MANIPULATE THOSE SHE CARES FOR IN ORDER TO KEEP THEM CLOSE TO HER OUT OF FEAR OF BEING LEFT BEHIND. SHE IS A REMINDER TO LOVE FREELY WITHOUT CONDITIONS AND TO LOVE BOLDLY, CASTING ASIDE THE FEAR OF BEING ALONE.

THE DREAMER

KEYWORDS: CREATIVE, ORIGINAL, UNFOCUSED

WHETHER AWAKE OR ASLEEP, THE IMAGINATION IS THE DREAMER'S PLAYGROUND. CREATIVE AND INVENTIVE, THE DREAMER'S STRONG POINT IS THINKING OUTSIDE THE BOX.

THE DREAMER CAN SPEND HOURS LOST IN THOUGHT INVENTING RICH WORLDS, UNIQUE SCENARIOS, AND APPROACHING PROBLEMS WITH THE GIFT OF UNCONVENTIONAL THINKING.

HAVING A RICH IMAGINATION COMBINED WITH THE ABILITY TO FIND CONTENTMENT IN DREAMING, OR DAYDREAMING, MAKES THE DREAMER ONE OF THE MOST CREATIVE INCARNATIONS.

THE GREATEST CHALLENGE FOR THE DREAMER IS FINDING THE FOCUS TO BRING IDEAS TO FRUITION.

THE
GHOST

THE GHOST

KEYWORDS: HAUNTING, FADED, NEBULOUS

A DREAM FORGOTTEN? A CRUCIAL THOUGHT LOST TO THE HUSTLE AND BUSTLE OF LIFE? THESE ARE THE DOMAIN OF THE GHOST.

OFTEN, WE RETAIN ONLY IMPRESSIONS OF OUR DREAMS OR DAYDREAMS. WE AWAKEN, ONLY TO HAVE OUR MINDS WIPED CLEAR OF WHATEVER MESSAGE WAS CAREFULLY DELIVERED TO US. AT OTHER TIMES, OUR DREAMS ARE CRISP AND CLEAR AS DAYLIGHT, BUT THE MESSAGE IS STILL LOST, AND SOME CRUCIAL DETAIL FORGOTTEN. IN THESE WAYS, OUR DREAMS BECOME GHOSTS. ONLY THROUGH CAREFUL AND TIMELY (OFTEN IMMEDIATE) EXAMINATION OF OUR SLEEPING VISIONS CAN WE JOURNEY THROUGH THE FOG AND ARRIVE AT WHAT OUR MINDS ARE TRYING HARD TO TELL US.

IF THE GHOST TOUCHES YOU, AN OPPORTUNITY TO FOCUS IS AT HAND.

THE
HEALER

THE HEALER

KEYWORDS: HOPE, RADIANCE, EXPERIENCE

THE HEALER EMBODIES HOPE. ARMED WITH THE INTIMATE KNOWLEDGE OF PERSONAL WOUNDS AND STRUGGLES, THE HEALER IS ABLE TO TRANSMUTE THE ENERGY OF HARDSHIPS INTO HEALING LIGHT. WITH THIS ABILITY, THE INTIMATE KNOWLEDGE OF PAINFUL EXPERIENCES IS USED TO HELP OTHERS THROUGH THE PROCESS OF THEIR OWN HEALING.

AN INSTINCT OF THE HEALER MAY BE TO "FIX" ANOTHER PERSON'S PROBLEMS BY DOING THE HEALING WORK FOR THEM OUT OF COMPASSION. DO NOT TAKE ANOTHER PERSON'S PAIN AND STRUGGLES AS YOUR OWN. INSTEAD, ALLOW YOURSELF TO BE A LIGHT IN THE DARKNESS – A RADIANT EXAMPLE OF HEALING AND HOPE THAT COMES WITH TIME, PERSEVERANCE, AND THE DEVELOPMENT OF INNER STRENGTH.

THE
ILLUSIONIST

THE ILLUSIONIST

KEYWORDS: TRICKSTER, IMPOSTER, PERFORMER

TO THE ILLUSIONIST, THE WORLD IS A PLAYGROUND WITHOUT LIMITS. TO POSSESS AN EVER-CHANGING PERSONALITY, TO MIMIC THE FASHIONS OF OTHERS, AND TO DISCONNECT FROM ONE'S TRUE SELF IN ORDER TO BECOME SOMEONE NEW, THESE ARE THE WAYS THE ILLUSIONIST SURVIVES — AND THRIVES. IT'S PROBABLE WE ALL KNOW A PERSON LIKE THIS IN OUR LIVES. AND FOR SOME OF US, WE *ARE* THIS PERSON.

THE ILLUSIONIST WILL KNOWINGLY ALTER THEIR PERSONALITY IN THE MANNER OF A CHAMELEON, AND WILL PRESENT THEMSELVES AS SOMETHING OTHER THAN AUTHENTIC, USUALLY FOR PERSONAL GAIN. IN SOME CASES, THIS IS HARMLESS (EXCEPT TO THE ILLUSIONIST THEMSELVES) OR EVEN ENTERTAINING. AND YET, EVERY ACTION HAS A COST. TO LIVE A LIFE OF PRETENSE IS PERHAPS THE GREATEST SELF-BETRAYAL POSSIBLE.

THE
JESTER

THE JESTER

KEYWORDS: HUMOR, IRREVERENCE, RIDICULE

THE JESTER IS A NATURAL ENTERTAINER WHO IS GIFTED AT USING HUMOR IN MULTIPLE WAYS: TO BREAK DOWN BARRIERS, LIGHTEN A MOOD OR ATMOSPHERE, OR SIMPLY ENTERTAIN PEOPLE AND MAKE THEM LAUGH.

THE JESTER CAN OFTEN BE FOUND IN A GROUP SETTING PLAYING THE ROLE OF COMIC RELIEF. HAVING A LIGHTHEARTED CHARACTER GRANTS THE JESTER THE ABILITY TO USE SATIRE TO ILLUMINATE HYPOCRISY OR INJUSTICE.

THE JESTER MUST BE CAREFUL NOT TO USE HUMOR IN A PASSIVE AGGRESSIVE MANNER THAT RIDICULES, MOCKS, OR EVEN BULLIES BECAUSE IT MAY LEAD TO ALIENATION FROM OTHERS.

THE
NOVICE

THE NOVICE

KEYWORDS: NAIVE, OPTIMISTIC, CURIOUS

WITH WIDE-EYED OPTIMISM AND A FEARLESS SENSE OF ADVENTURE, THE NOVICE EXEMPLIFIES LIMITLESS POTENTIAL, AND THE INFINITE POSSIBILITIES LIFE CAN OFFER.

THE NOVICE IS NOT LADEN WITH FEARS OF FAILURE, DANGER, OR LOSS, BUT IS MOTIVATED BY CURIOSITY AND INNOCENCE.

THE NOVICE REPRESENTS THE EXCITEMENT THAT COMES WITH NEW BEGINNINGS. NO MATTER WHAT AGE WE ARE, WE CAN EMBODY THIS FEARLESS NATURE AND ENTHUSIASTICALLY EMBRACE A NEW START IN LIFE. WHILE INNOCENCE IS A KEY CHARACTERISTIC OF THE NOVICE, IT MAY BE DAMAGED BY UNANTICIPATED DISAPPOINTMENTS OR FAILURES IN LIFE. THE STRUGGLE FOR THE NOVICE IS TO MAINTAIN OPTIMISM IN THE FACE OF ADVERSITY.

THE
PHILOSOPHER

THE PHILOSOPHER

KEYWORDS: INTELLECTUAL, THEORIST, DETACHMENT

THE PHILOSOPHER IS THE THINKER WITHIN US ALL. TO DECIPHER NOT JUST HOW THE WORLD OPERATES, BUT ALSO WHY, IS THE PHILOSOPHER'S MOTIVATION (AND POSSIBLY LIFELONG STRUGGLE.) TO SEEK ANSWERS IS PERHAPS THE MOST HUMAN THING WE CAN DO. THE DESIRE NOT JUST FOR KNOWLEDGE, BUT FOR A DEEPER CONNECTION TO THAT KNOWLEDGE, CAN BE A NOBLE IF NOT ESSENTIAL, PURSUIT. KNOWLEDGE IS POWER, AFTER ALL.

SOMETIMES, THE PHILOSOPHER MIGHT DWELL TOO LONG IN THOUGHT. IF HARD-WON ANSWERS LEAD ONLY TO MORE QUESTIONS, THE TENDENCY CAN BE TO FALL EVER DEEPER INTO THE RABBIT HOLE OF THOUGHT INSTEAD OF ACTION.

THE PHILOSOPHER LIVES IN ALL OF US, AND IS A REMINDER OF OUR HUMAN NEED TO SEEK THE TRUTH OF OUR EXISTENCE.

THE

PHOENIX

THE PHOENIX

KEYWORDS: REINVENTION, RENEWAL, METAMORPHOSIS

To reinvent one's self, to become new, to let go of useless ideas and obsolete self-images, these are the ways of the phoenix. The remnants of yesterday will burn by the fire of the phoenix's wings, and a new life will emerge.

The phoenix's life isn't easy, but can be exceptionally rewarding nonetheless. Deep and meaningful reinventions of one's self may be necessary and happen multiple times throughout a lifetime. If done with forethought and sincerity, these changes may lead us to become better, wiser, and happier.

But a word of caution. Though the phoenix may smolder and be reborn, it is entirely possible to re-emerge into a life little better (or even worse) than before. —For wherever the phoenix flies, no matter how far removed from its previous life, it must still contend with being itself.

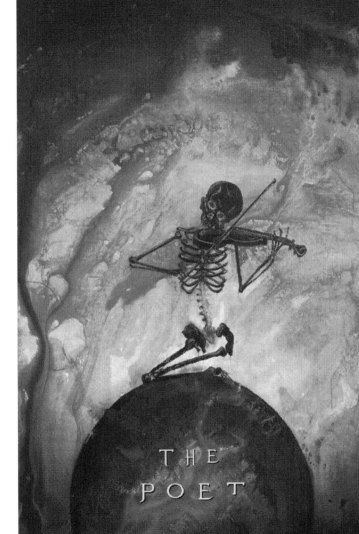

THE
POET

THE POET

KEYWORDS: ROMANTIC, EXPRESSIVE, ARTISTIC

TO THE POET, EMOTIONS ARE INFLATED, EVEN EXALTED. QUIXOTIC, THE POET IS IN LOVE WITH FALLING IN LOVE. THE IDEALIZATION OF ROMANCE CAN BE A FIXATION FOR THE POET. IF A ROMANTIC EXPERIENCE FAILS TO BE ANYTHING LESS THAN PERFECT, THE POET IS DEFLATED AND QUICK TO MOVE ON TO OTHER ROMANTIC PURSUITS.

EXPRESSING EMOTIONS IS A NECESSITY IN THE POET'S LIFE. THROUGH MUSIC OR OTHER ARTISTIC MEANS, THE POET IS ABLE TO POUR HIS PASSION INTO SOMETHING MORE SATISFYING THAN THE PURSUIT OF PERFECT ROMANTIC LOVE.

THE POET IS A REMINDER TO MAKE TIME FOR CREATIVE EXPRESSION IN YOUR LIFE.

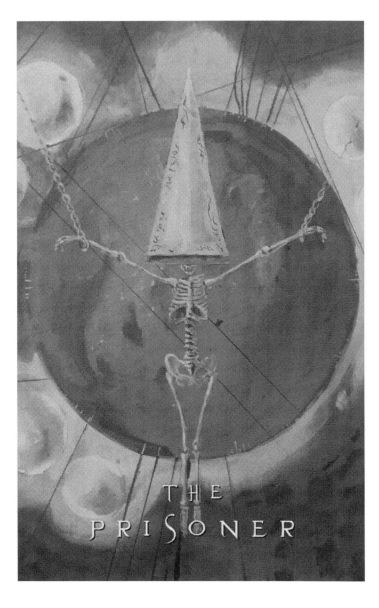

THE PRISONER

KEYWORDS: COMPULSION, NEGATIVITY, CYCLES

THE PRISONER IS ONE WHO FINDS THEMSELVES LOCKED BEHIND THE BARS OF A NEGATIVE THOUGHT CYCLE. AT SOME POINT, THE PRISONER BECOMES STUCK IN A PATTERN (OR SEVERAL PATTERNS) OF AN UNHEALTHY LIFE. THE HABITS VARY WIDELY (ALCOHOL, DRUGS, GAMBLING, ETC.) BUT THE CAUSE IS OFTEN THE SAME.

BEING SUBTLER THAN ANY PHYSICAL CONFINEMENT, THE PRISON OF THE MIND CAN PROVE DIFFICULT TO ESCAPE. MANY KEYS MAY BE NEEDED TO FINALLY UNLOCK THE DOOR AND LET THE LIGHT BACK IN.

HOWEVER, IF THE NEGATIVE STATE OF MIND CAN BE SHATTERED, THE PRISONER WILL FIND THEMSELVES UNSHACKLED, FREE TO LIVE UNBOUND BY DEPENDENCY, AND POSSIBLY STRONGER THAN EVER.

THE PRISONER REMINDS US TO BREAK NEGATIVE THOUGHT PATTERNS AS SOON AS THEY ARISE, AND TO SEEK HELP SHOULD THEY RUN TOO DEEP.

THE

REFLECTION

THE REFLECTION

KEYWORDS: MIRROR, ILLUMINATION, DISILLUSION

THE REFLECTION IS AN IMAGE OF YOURSELF CAST BACK AT YOU THROUGH THE EYES OF THE PEOPLE IN YOUR LIFE. IT IS A LIVING MIRROR THAT BRINGS ILLUMINATION, HELPS DISPEL ILLUSIONS, AND ALLOWS YOU TO SEE YOURSELF FROM OTHER PERSPECTIVES.

NOTICE HOW OTHERS REACT TO YOU OR CHANGE IN YOUR PRESENCE. YOU MAY LEARN ABOUT YOUR IMPACT ON THE WORLD THROUGH THE EYES OF THE PEOPLE AROUND YOU. DON'T JUDGE YOURSELF OR YOUR WORTH BASED ON WHAT OTHER PEOPLE THINK OF YOU. THE REFLECTION IS NOT ABOUT CHANGING WHO YOU ARE; RATHER, IT CAN OPEN YOUR EYES TO REVELATIONS THAT BRING A GREATER SENSE OF SELF-AWARENESS.

THE
SAGE

THE SAGE

KEYWORDS: TEACHER, GUIDE, WISDOM

THE SAGE, WISEST AMONG US, KEEPER OF KNOWLEDGE, IS A SACRED ROLE. —FOR WHAT WOULD WE BE WITHOUT TEACHERS, WITHOUT CALM AND KNOWLEDGEABLE HANDS TO GUIDE US INTO THE UNKNOWN?

A TRUE SAGE WILL GIVE FORTH IDEAS AND ADVICE WITHOUT NEED OF COMPENSATION. IF AN ELDER AMONG US (OR SOMETIMES EVEN A YOUNG, YET WISE SOUL) TAKES IT UPON THEMSELVES TO BESTOW KNOWLEDGE, IT BECOMES SOMETHING TO BE TREASURED. THE GIFT OF KNOWLEDGE GIVEN IN EARNEST HAS NO EQUAL.

HOWEVER, SEEKING THE WISDOM OF A SAGE HAS ITS RISKS. NOT ALL KNOWLEDGE IS GIVEN WITH A PURE HEART, AND DISPENSERS OF UNSOLICITED/UNNEEDED/UNTRUE ADVICE MAY SEEM AS THOUGH THEY ARE WISE, BUT IN FACT MAY HAVE PRIVATE MOTIVATIONS.

THE SAGE IS A REMINDER THAT WITH GREAT KNOWLEDGE COMES GREAT RESPONSIBILITY.

THE
SLEEPWALKER

THE SLEEPWALKER

KEYWORDS: NUMB, DISENGAGED, INDIFFERENT

THE SLEEPWALKER MOVES THROUGH THE DAYS WITHOUT ENGAGING DIRECTLY IN LIFE. PERHAPS BECAUSE OF PAST TRAUMA, PERHAPS DUE TO MALAISE OR LACK OF STIMULATION, ONE WHO IS SLEEPWALKING GOES THROUGH THE MOTIONS, DETACHED AND AIMLESS, SIMPLY SURVIVING ONE DAY TO THE NEXT.

TO SLEEPWALK IS TO BE NUMB IN MIND, BODY, AND SPIRIT. EVEN THOUGH ONE IS TECHNICALLY AWAKE, AWARENESS AND CONSCIOUSNESS ARE SUBDUED. SOMETIMES, THIS STATE OF MIND EXISTS WHILE THE SLEEPWALKER IS COMPLETELY OBLIVIOUS. YEARS CAN PASS, EVEN LIFETIMES.

ANYONE CAN EXPERIENCE PERIODS OF LIFE DURING WHICH THEY SLEEPWALK. THE KEY TO REAWAKENING IS RECOGNIZING THAT ONE HAS DETACHED FROM LIFE. SELF-AWARENESS IS OF UTMOST IMPORTANCE. ONLY THEN CAN THE SLEEPWALKER RISE.

THE
STAG

THE STAG

KEYWORDS: VIGILANT, CARING, PROTECTOR

THE STAG POSSESSES THE ENERGY OF A LEADER AND IS A FIGURE WHO IS FIERCELY PROTECTIVE OF THE CREATURES AND LAND HE OVERSEES. VIGILANT AND CARING, HE IS A GUIDE AND SHIELD FOR THOSE UNDER HIS CARE.

THE STAG IS A REMINDER THAT, WHEN IN A LEADERSHIP POSITION, ONE SHOULD LEAD JUSTLY AND NOT MISUSE A POSITION OF POWER WHICH CAN LEAD TO THE OPPRESSION OF THOSE WHO RELY ON HIM, RATHER THAN MAKING THEM FEEL SECURE.

THE
TRAVELER

THE TRAVELER

KEYWORDS: COLLECTOR, TRANSITORY, NOMAD

THE TRAVELER EXPRESSES THE ENERGY OF IMPERMANENCE. A COLLECTOR OF EXPERIENCES, RELATIONSHIPS, OR FRIENDSHIPS, THE TRAVELER PREFERS TO STAY IN MOTION.

A DRIFTER WHO QUICKLY PASSES THROUGH JOBS, RELATIONSHIPS, AND LIVING SPACES, THE TRAVELER DEPENDS ON AN ABUNDANCE OF FLEETING, EXTRINSIC EXPERIENCES TO CONSTRUCT THE INNER LANDSCAPE OF THE SELF. REMAINING STILL IS WASTED TIME AND MISSED OPPORTUNITIES.

WHILE DIFFERENT EXPERIENCES HELP CREATE A FULL LIFE AND ARE NECESSARY FOR PERSONAL GROWTH, THE TRAVELER CAN GET CAUGHT UP IN ENDLESS SEEKING OR EVEN AIMLESS WANDERING, NOT SETTLING FOR FEAR OF BEING STUCK. IT IS IMPORTANT TO TAKE TIME TO STAY STILL AND ALLOW YOURSELF TIME CONNECT TO MOMENTS DEEPLY AND FULLY WITHOUT CONSIDERING THE NEXT MOVE.

THE VICTIM

KEYWORDS: EXPECTATIONS, SELF-LIMITING, RESCUER

—FOR THE VICTIM INCARNATION, THE ATTACKER IS ONE'S OWN MIND AND THE RESISTANCE TO LET GO OF NEGATIVE SELF-PERCEPTIONS AND INHIBITING THOUGHT PATTERNS THAT CAUSE GREAT HARM.

BEING CLOAKED IN THE SHADOW OF LOW EXPECTATIONS OF YOURSELF MAY FEEL LIKE A COMFORTABLE WAY TO AVOID DISAPPOINTMENT OR KEEP FROM EXPOSING VULNERABILITY, BUT IT ONLY SUFFOCATES THE CRIES OF THE UNBOUND SELF.

UNDOING THE CONSTRUCTION OF SELF-LIMITING THOUGHTS REQUIRES A REVERSAL OF SELF-IMAGE AND DEMANDS CONFIDENCE AND GREAT STRENGTH OF MIND. IN ORDER TO ACCOMPLISH THIS, YOU MUST DECIDE TO BECOME YOUR OWN RESCUER.

THE
VISIONARY

THE VISIONARY

KEYWORDS: INVENTIVE, INSPIRED, MOTIVATED

THE VISIONARY IS SOMEONE WHO TURNS DREAMS INTO REALITY. —FROM TIME TO TIME, EVERY PERSON ALIVE WILL SPEAK THE WORDS, "I WISH..." BUT THE VISIONARY HAS A TALENT FOR GIVING THESE WISHES SUBSTANCE. THERE ARE NO DESIRES TOO LARGE OR SMALL, NO MOUNTAIN THAT CANNOT BE SCALED.

IN A VISIONARY'S MIND, THE FUTURE IS CREATED BY THE BUILDING BLOCKS OF THE PRESENT. SELF-MOTIVATED, THEY HAVE THE FORESIGHT, FOCUS, AND WILLPOWER TO VISUALIZE A DESIRE AND SHAPE THEIR WORLD AROUND IT.

OF COURSE, NOT ALL VISIONS ARE MADE EQUAL. POSSESSING THE WILL TO CREATE SOMETHING NEW DOESN'T ALWAYS TAKE ETHICS OR THE NEEDS OF OTHERS INTO CONSIDERATION. —FOR THESE REASONS, THE VISIONARY FACES THE CHALLENGE OF LEAVING THE WORLD BETTER THAN WHEN THEY FOUND IT.

THE VISIONARY REMINDS US THAT TRULY, DREAMS CAN BECOME REAL.

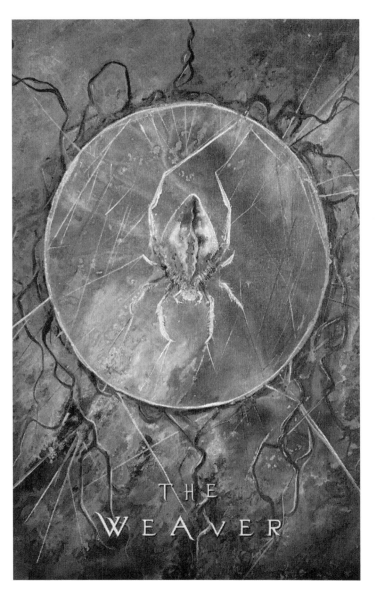

THE

WEAVER

THE WEAVER

KEYWORDS: AUTHOR, DESTINY, ADAPTABLE

THE WEAVER IS ONE WHO LEAVES LITTLE TO CHANCE. THE WEB OF A WEAVER'S LIFE STORY CAN BE DESCRIBED AS BEING MADE OF CAREFULLY PLACED THREADS, EACH LINE WOVEN WITH GREAT DETERMINATION. IF ANY ONE PART OF THEIR WEB IS DAMAGED, THEY WILL ADAPT AND REPAIR THE THREAD, EMBRACING THE ADJUSTMENT WITH EASE.

IN BEING THE AUTHOR OF THEIR OWN LIFE STORY, THE WEAVER IS THE ESSENCE OF SELF-CONTROL AND WILL OFTEN SEEM TO OTHERS AS HONEST AND GENUINE. AFTER ALL, THE STRONGEST WEBS ARE MADE OF TRUTH.

IN CONSTRUCTING AN IDEAL LIFE, THE WEAVER MUST REMEMBER THAT NOT ALL EVENTS CAN BE CONTROLLED, AND THAT SOME THREADS IN LIFE ARE MEANT TO BE USED, THEN RELEASED INTO THE WIND. SERENDIPITOUS MOMENTS AND CHANCE ENCOUNTERS WILL OCCUR, AND SHOULD BE EMBRACED, EVEN WHEN THE WEB SEEMS UNPREPARED TO CATCH THEM.

THE WEAVER TEACHES US THAT WITH PREPARATION AND INTENT, OUR LIVES CAN TAKE THE SAME SHAPE AS OUR DESIRES.

TRANSFORMATION

TRANSFORMATION

KEYWORDS: SNAKE, ASCEND, AWAKENING

THE SERPENT SYMBOLIZES PERSONAL TRANSFORMATION AND AWAKENING TO A HIGHER CONSCIOUSNESS. IT SIGNIFIES THE CYCLE OF SHEDDING THE OLD AND SUCCESSFULLY TRANSITIONING INTO A NEW CHAPTER OF LIFE.

IF POSITIVE TRANSFORMATION ARRIVES, ONE MUST BE PREPARED TO NOT ONLY GREET THEIR NEW LIFE WITH OPEN ARMS, BUT ALSO TO ALLOW THE PAST TO BE SET ASIDE.

MAINTAIN ONLY THE HABITS AND RITUALS WHICH BRING HEALTH AND HARMONY. ALLOW ALL ELSE TO FALL AWAY.

TRAPPED

KEYWORDS: CONFINED, STUCK, REPETITIVE

TRAPPED IS BEING STUCK IN REPETITION — THE SAME LIFE
CHOICES CREATE THE SAME RESULTS IN A SEEMINGLY
ENDLESS CYCLE. IT CAN SEEM ALL BUT IMPOSSIBLE TO
BREAK THROUGH.

YOUR OPTIONS TO ESCAPE MAY SEEM LIMITED OR
NONEXISTENT, BUT NEGATIVE THOUGHT-CYCLES SIMPLY
MUST BE BROKEN. THE SITUATION MUST BE VIEWED FROM
A NEW ANGLE IN ORDER TO SEE A CLEAR WAY OUT.

SEEK THE WISDOM OF FRIENDS AND LOVED ONES, AND BE
OPEN TO ALL POSSIBLE SOLUTIONS, EVEN THOSE WHICH
SEEM INTIMIDATING.

WATER

WATER

KEYWORDS: PLACID, CHANGEABLE, CONTENT

WATER IS EMOTIONAL CONTENTMENT. IT IS A REMINDER THAT THE ABILITY TO VIEW EMOTIONS AS TEMPORARY AND CHANGEABLE CAN BRING INNER PEACE DURING TEMPESTUOUS TIMES.

THE ABILITY TO REMAIN FLUID AND THE WILLINGNESS TO FLOW WITH RAPID CHANGES RATHER THAN RESIST THEM IS IMPORTANT FOR RESILIENCE. INNER PEACE AND CONTENTMENT IN THE FACE OF ANY ADVERSITY WILL BRING TRIUMPH.

WINDOW

WINDOW

KEYWORDS: OUTLOOK, INSIGHT, PERSPECTIVE

THE TWO WAYS OF LOOKING THROUGH A WINDOW, LOOKING IN OR LOOKING OUT, REPRESENT DIFFERENT PERSPECTIVES. WHETHER DREAMED OR DAYDREAMED OF, WINDOWS CAN SYMBOLIZE PATHWAYS TO HIGHER OR DIFFERENT LEVELS OF CONSCIOUSNESS.

BY VIEWING THE WORLD FROM BEHIND A LITERAL OR FIGURATIVE PANE OF GLASS, WE KEEP OURSELVES SEPARATE FROM THE OUTSIDE REALM, DISALLOWING THE POSSIBILITY OF INTERACTING WITH THE REAL WORLD. ALTERNATIVELY, THE WINDOW MAY BE SYMBOLIC OF SELF-REFLECTION, IN THAT THE PLACES WE SEE BEYOND THE GLASS ARE NOT OUTSIDE REALMS, BUT A GLIMPSE OF OUR TRUE SELVES.

LOOK CLOSELY, AND DETERMINE WHETHER WHAT YOU SEE IS OF THE OUTSIDE WORLD, OR A VIEW OF YOURSELF FROM A NEW PERSPECTIVE.

J Edward & Heather Neill

HAUNTED
CAT
TAROT

A Tarot Guidebook

Spirits & Shadows

Shadows

An Oracle Deck

J Edward & Heather Neill

Wisdom of the Raven

OF

THE RAVEN

AN ORACLE DECK

Shadow Journey Tarot

J Edward & Heather Neill

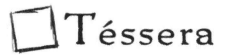

Made in the USA
Columbia, SC
14 November 2024

46283544R00063